Wheels Around Dunfermline and West Fife

by
Alan Brotchie

A rail-level view taken inside the north cantilever of the Forth Bridge in the late 1920s showing a fish train heading south hauled by the former North British Railway locomotive *Glen Lyon*.

The publishers regret that they cannot supply
copies of any pictures featured in this book.

ACKNOWLEDGEMENTS

With thanks to George Beattie, David Beveridge, Harry Jack, George Robertson, Eric Simpson, Dunfermline Library and West Fife Museums Service.

The elegant lines of the Forth Rail Bridge are seen to good effect from the deck of one of the vehicle ferries that formerly operated on this crossing. Its massive scale can be gauged by comparison with the diminutive passenger train heading to Fife. These two ferry boats, *Robert the Bruce* and *Queen Margaret*, were put in service during 1934 and generally passed each other in the middle of the passage between North and South Queensferry. They were later to be joined by two more similar vessels until all were supplanted by the Forth Road Bridge in 1964. On this occasion the ferry is carrying little vehicular traffic. When it sailed close to the rail bridge its passengers had to be wary of coins thrown from passing trains for good luck. Many of these coins never reached the water, but instead formed extra income for the bridge workers who collected them! This custom doesn't seem to have survived the change from steam trains to diesel multiple units.

INTRODUCTION

Dunfermline, sitting astride a strategic route from Edinburgh to northern Scotland by way of the Queen's Ferry and Perth, would have been one of the first places in the realm to witness the increasing use of wheeled transport as change slowly occurred during the Middle Ages. Such change was, however, effectively restrained by the poor state of the road network which was initially only suitable for packhorse travel. So inadequate were the roads that transporting goods in anything other than the smallest quantities would generally be done using coastal vessels, a practice that accounts for the numerous small harbours found at frequent intervals around the coast of the 'Kingdom of Fife'.

During the late eighteenth and early nineteenth centuries the traditionally agricultural nature of Fife gave way to an industrial economy in many southern parts of the county, based on the exploitation of coal and ironstone reserves. Transport of these commodities to the sea for export – or for home consumption elsewhere – meant that this part of Scotland was amongst the earliest to use primitive waggonways, whereby a horse, pulling four-wheeled waggons along wooden rails, could increase its load by a factor of six. The first waggonways in the area were built to serve Lord Elgin's lime works at Charlestown, delivering coal to the works from inland collieries. Early waggonways with wooden rails were also built in Pittenweem, Leven, Wemyss and around Dunfermline, where the largest accumulation of different lines were to be found, with at least six belonging to various coal proprietors.

Turnpike road trusts were set up in the early nineteenth century, collecting tolls from road-users to pay for the upkeep and improvement of the road network, and these trusts did indeed improve roads, and in some instances construct new ones. Local examples of this enlightened system can be seen in the efforts of the trust in upgrading the Great North Road north of Inverkeithing, as well as the Outh & Nivingston Trust's improvement of the road past the modern Knockhill racetrack.

'Proper' railways developed from primitive wooden waggonways with iron, then steel, taking the place of wood for rails and wheels – another leap forward in efficiency. Steam locomotives replaced horses, the first 'iron horse' in use locally being seen on the Dunfermline to Stirling Railway in 1849. Soon Dunfermline was joined to the emerging national rail network, and as exploitation of west Fife's coal resources took hold the town became a major railway (and road) junction, with routes radiating to all points of the compass.

In common with many other population centres of a similar size, a carriage-building industry developed as communications improved. In Dunfermline's case this was to lead to the construction of one of the very earliest motor vehicles. Michael Tod & Sons of the Devon Engine Works, Campbell Street (better known then as bleachfield engineers) built a three-wheeled car in 1897 with bodywork by George Kay & Son of Inglis Street. Remarkably this unique vehicle (no more were built) survived in Kay's workshop until the 1960s, when the engine was rescued and taken to Glasgow's Museum of Transport.

'Modern' transport in the shape of electric trams came to the area in 1909 and served Dunfermline for nearly 30 years before being ousted by motor buses. Road transport became the preferred means of getting around from the 1930s, with the local railways losing their grip on short distance travel.

After the cessation of deep coal mining in the 1960s, most local railway branch lines were lifted. Coal from opencast sites was – and is still – generally carried by motor lorry, when it could be more economically and safely transported by rail were the facility still available. Some of the coal required by Longannet power station is carried by rail to this day, and hopefully the percentage will increase following the reopening of the rail link from the west, thus removing a proportion of lorries from the already congested roads.

Motorway construction to the east of Dunfermline has been the latest manifestation of the transport revolution. Now, instead of the town being at the centre of a network, as it was in the days of the turnpike road system, it is effectively out on a limb, with most vehicles and their occupants bypassing the centre. They don't know what they are missing!

Dunfermline is at present expanding rapidly to the east in a seemingly unrelenting succession of suburban developments which would be equally at home on the outskirts of Milton Keynes or Surbiton. The inhabitants of these dwellings are, in many cases, Edinburgh-bound commuters adding to the stream of traffic on the already overloaded road leading to Scotland's capital. Hopefully in time most will come to realise that Scotland's former capital has much to offer both in terms of employment opportunities and leisure facilities.

Cycling became a popular leisure pastime following the development of the modern bicycle by a Scot, Gavin Dalziel of Lesmahagow, in the 1840s. The principle of two-wheeled velocipedes actually dated back to the previous century, and the appearance of an early machine, described as a 'dandy-charger', was sufficiently novel to be reported in an Edinburgh newspaper in 1817! The Cyclists' Touring Club, founded in 1878, initially had a uniform for its members, but this had fallen out of favour by the time this photograph of members of the Dunfermline branch was taken on a 1926 outing to Dollar. Second from the left is John Edward Aloysius Steggall who was Professor of Applied Mathematics at University College Dundee from 1895 to 1933. An enthusiastic cyclist, he made the round trip of 500 miles from Dundee to Cardiff at the age of 65 to attend a meeting of the British Association for the Advancement of Science. In front of him is Miss Pearl Fraser, wearing the latest cycling fashion – 'rationals'!

The first town of any size encountered on the journey north into Fife, either by road or by rail, is Inverkeithing, where this remarkable view, one of a pair forming a stereographic photograph (designed to give a 3D effect when seen through a special viewer), was captured over 100 years ago. While the time of day can be accurately pinpointed to 1.15 from the clock on the Town House, no clue is given as to the precise year. It would seem that one of the young ladies in the centre of the scene is being taught how to ride a bicycle, not an activity which would be actively encouraged in the traffic of today! The gas lamp provides a convenient rest for the youth on the left to enjoy the spectacle. Gas lighting was introduced into the burgh in 1843 from a small gasworks constructed near the harbour. Despite the best efforts of the local council, Inverkeithing never became a coal exporting port to rival those both up and down the Forth. The denial of this source of income was a constant source of irritation to Inverkeithing's burgh treasurer.

HIGH STREET AND PARISH CHURCH, INVERKEITHING.

This view of Inverkeithing High Street – part of the Great North Road – can be confidently dated to the summer of 1924. The open AEC charabanc in the centre belonged to the Saline Motor Service which ran to and from Dunfermline, a route which might have been upgraded to tramway operation but for the intervention of the First World War. Behind the bus is the fourteenth century tower of the later Parish Church of St Peter which still dominates the north end of the High Street. In 1758 Inverkeithing was described as a 'mean, miserable and paltry town', a sweeping generalisation that today's residents would no doubt fiercely disagree with.

Until very recently, Caldwell's Paper Mill was the largest employer in Inverkeithing. The works, established in 1894 by brothers Alfred and Gordon Caldwell, suffered a major setback following a disastrous fire on 24 May 1913. However, within a year a completely reconstructed mill was in production featuring the latest paper-making machinery. Caldwell's relied to a large degree on supplies arriving by rail (and through Inverkeithing harbour), and this view shows the mill's steam 'puggie', which was used for shunting in the company's yard. This little tank was purchased following reconstruction of the works after the fire. It should have been a bargain, as Barclay of Kilmarnock seem to have built (or rebuilt) it from an assortment of parts of older locomotives. If there were earlier locos used at Caldwell's mill they have not been traced, but this was the first of several. Diesel traction replaced steam in 1950 until rail traffic ceased in 1973.

To ensure that they had an adequate supply of railway waggons for their needs, Caldwell's purchased their own rolling stock, liveried with the company name and for their use only. Whilst this ensured there were enough waggons available, the system (which was widely adopted) resulted in much wasted effort in returning empty waggons to their owners, and eventually, during wartime, a 'common user' system was introduced to do away with this practice. This 'private owner' waggon was one of two built in 1900 for Caldwell by R. Y. Pickering & Co. of Wishaw. In later years second-hand trucks were purchased from the Admiralty at Rosyth.

Looking south along Alma Street in Inverkeithing, with a two-wheeled delivery cart standing, sensibly, across the slope. This was then the main road to Kirkcaldy and the east, and the dip down to cross the Keithing Burn created quite a stiff gradient for horse traffic. Crossing the street at the foot of the hill was the route of the Halbeath waggonway, built in the 1780s to take coal from collieries at Halbeath (and later Townhill) either to Inverkeithing harbour or to a pier built by the Halbeath company for their own use at the East Ness. While Dunrobin Cottage (right) still exists – albeit considerably altered – none of the old cottages beyond have survived the passage of time.

Major excavation works under way near Burntisland in 1906/7, probably in connection with siding extensions. Large numbers of navvies were employed on the project, digging and loading by hand the one-horse tipping carts. Each individual would own his own shovel, which was kept in good condition by him and travelled with him from job to job. On the higher level there runs a temporary lightly constructed railway, with one of the contractor's waggons visible behind the men in the centre of the photograph. To the right, sporting bowler hat, stands an authoritative figure, possibly the engineer or foreman.

Burntisland's Alcan aluminium works was the town's principal employer from 1917 to 2003, and almost to the end of its existence was dependent to a large degree on rail transport. Raw bauxite – averaging 150,000 tons annually – was brought to the harbour and then taken in trainloads to the works. The bright red residue (which seemed to have no commercial value) which remained after completion of the extraction process was then dumped, first in the shallow bay where the old Sea Mill formerly stood, then below the Binn Hill, as evidenced by the characteristic red-stained roads on its approaches. The plant was served by three diminutive shunting pugs (two of which are seen here), all of which survived to be taken into preservation.

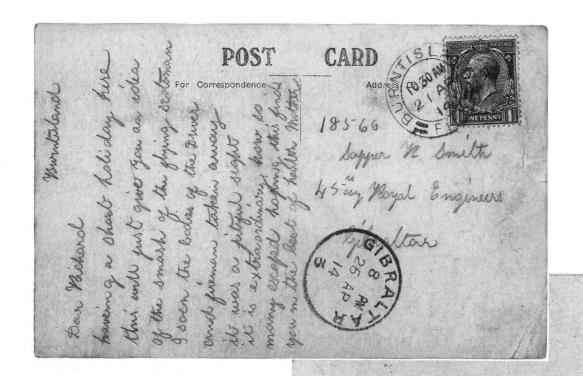

Burntisland

Dear Richard
having a short holiday here
this will just give you an idea
of the smash of the flying scotsman
I seen the bodes of the driver
and fireman taken away
it was a pitiful sight
it is extraordinary how so
many escaped hoping this finds
you in the best of health Willie

POST CARD

For Correspondence

Address

18566
Sapper W. Smith
45ᵗᵘ Royal Engineers
Gibraltar

One of the worst accidents to occur on the North British Railway happened on 14 April 1914 when the express from London and Edinburgh to Dundee and Aberdeen collided with a shunting goods train just north of Burntisland station at 4.30 a.m., the result of an error by a signalman. Lives lost were restricted to the driver and fireman of the London train, as described by the sender of this postcard, which remarkably took just four days reach its destination in Gibraltar.

Recovery of the locomotive *Auld Reekie* from where it had embedded itself in the Links proved a difficult task. Having returned it to a vertical position, a short length of temporary track was laid from the main line. The badly damaged engine was then dragged up this by no fewer than four locomotives, as seen in this view. After repair at Cowlairs works, Glasgow, it served without further incident until withdrawn from service in August 1935. In the background is the conical roof of Burntisland's roundhouse locomotive depot, formerly part of the headquarters of the Edinburgh & Northern Railway and a prominent landmark until its demolition in the 1930s when the locomotives were transferred to a newly enlarged depot at Thornton.

Burntisland's Links are more happily associated with the funfair, whose stance is close to where the 1914 accident took place, and which was more recently the location of a coal train derailment on 8 July 1998, the train almost landing on top of showmen's caravans parked making preparations for the shows. This August 1965 photograph shows Codona's 'Jet Planes' ride with a full complement of joyriders. Behind can be seen the bridge over the main line railway. Burntisland is a popular destination for west of Scotland holidaymakers, particularly at the time of the Glasgow Fair. Despite the appeal of cheap flights to the sun, it remains a favourite spot for a break.

In the 1950s and 1960s travelling fairs were a Mecca not only for pleasure-seekers, but also for the vintage vehicle enthusiast. Initially many showmen purchased second-hand Tilling Stevens buses, popular in the twenties and thirties with their unique petrol-electric drive, but these had generally completed their second lease of life by this period and been scrapped. A new generation of second-hand vehicles then took over, such as WG 5926, a 1937 Leyland formerly the property of W. Alexander & Co. of Falkirk, seen at Burntisland in 1965.

Interesting old commercial vehicles were also to be found owned by showmen. Seen here at Burntisland, with the Binn Hill as a backdrop to the Links, are Bob Lovett & Son's Atkinson (HOT 639) and Maudslay (KYK 354), again photographed in August 1965.

The wooden pier at Aberdour harbour forms the backdrop of this studio portrait produced by the Parisian Photo Company of Princes Street in Edinburgh. From left to right, the participants are Maggie Christie, Richard Birmingham, his brother Jack, and Aggie Gray, all from Dunfermline. The couples were later married (Richard and Maggie, Jack and Aggie). Aggie Birmingham was prominent for many years in the local musical society, while Richard later played a prominent role in Renfrew Town Council. Birmingham Road in Renfrew commemorates his period as 'Father of the Council' there.

A group of girls from Mathewson's Bothwell linen works in Elgin Street, Dunfermline, on an outing in 1916. The nationalistic photographer's studio scenery represents an aircraft – 'First Stop Berlin' – flying off to drop bombs on the Kaiser. After Berlin the troupe are going on for a 'Week-end Excursion to the North Pole & Up It'! They all look singularly underdressed for the occasion! Mathewson's works was a major employer in the area from 1865 to 1932, the former factory being demolished in the 1950s.

St Leonard's Hill House was the substantial home of the proprietor of St Leonard's Mill, Mr Erskine Beveridge. This charming view from *c*.1907 shows the head gardener, Mr Dalrymple, and his family. The area took its name from a chapel and hospital nearby which can be dated back as far back as 1272. The ruination of these buildings, begun during the Reformation in 1560, is said to have been completed by Cromwell's forces after the Battle of Pitreavie some 90 years later. St Leonard's works soon became a thing of wonder in its own right. Opened in June 1851, within 30 years it had over 1,200 employees working its steam-powered looms manufacturing damask (fine patterned linen used for tablecloths etc.), making it probably the largest mill of its type in the area. Beveridge obtained much of his steam plant (and many looms) from the failed Baldridge Works of Robert Robertson. Of Dunfermline's dozen such works, St Leonard's survived the longest, closing in December 1989 after 138 years of operation. The office and warehouse building has been reconstructed as flats, but the factory has been demolished.

In addition to being the proprietor of one of Dunfermline's aerated water factories, Gilbert Rae was a keen amateur photographer and also the owner of one of the first motor cars in the area, an 1898 Daimler. He took many photographs of his factory and the various vehicles owned by the company. The works at Golfdrum Street occupied part of the complex built in the 1840s as the Baldridge Mills. Much later they became known to enthusiasts and historians of vintage vehicles, and several of Mr Rae's old vehicles were eventually sold to John Sword, proprietor of the Western SMT Company. Some vehicles from that collection were acquired by Lord Elgin when, after John Sword's death, his collection was sold by auction. Gilbert Rae's first Daimler is now to be seen in Glasgow's Museum of Transport.

Dunfermline & West Fife Hospital.   Christie.

A horse-drawn delivery cart photographed in Reid Street at Nethertown Broad Street c.1910. The latter name was introduced in the early nineteenth century, the route previously being known as Geelie's Wynd (the wynd for the 'geelies' or abbey servants). Dunfermline & West Fife Hospital has now lost its caring role to the replacement Queen Margaret Hospital, with most of the older complex demolished in recent years, its place to be taken by new purpose-built offices for council officials. When the 'West Fife' was opened in 1894 – as the Cottage Hospital – it provided care for sixteen patients looked after by a staff of three. By the generosity of the widow of Andrew Carnegie, it was one of the first hospitals to be equipped with X-ray facilities.

Deliveries being made from David Allan's 'Hygienic' Bakery van in Charlestown in the 1900s. On the reverse of this old postcard a contemporary note reads: 'The shelves in the van are filled with bread (unwrapped), plain "halfs", pan "halfs" and French "halfs". The drawer underneath contained "tea bread" (sugar buns, plain buns and treacle cakes). The driver-vanman has just given the horse its feed bag, probably adjusted the traces, patted it on the neck, stroked it on the flanks and is now busy filling a customer's apron with cakes he has <u>lifted</u> out of the jumble in the drawer.' Next to the van is a water well, while the gates into Broomhall Estate are on the right. David Allan's bakery was located in the High Street, and its owner was a prime mover in the establishment of the Boy Scout movement in west Fife.

Although proposals for a tramway to link Dunfermline to the mining villages of west Fife were first aired in 1903, construction by the Edinburgh contractors Balfour Beatty Ltd. did not commence until the summer of 1909. Having started, no time was lost and 6½ miles of track-laying was completed in just over three months. A site for a depot was chosen near the middle of the route, at Woodend, Cowdenbeath, seen here during October 1909 with the first of the trams just visible on the right. The trucks for trams which have yet to arrive are in place while completion of the depot continues. One of the bowler-hatted gentlemen to the left is George Balfour, who later became an MP.

CAR TERMINUS TOWNHILL CHRISTIE

In addition to the main tramway line which linked Dunfermline to Cowdenbeath, Lochgelly, Glencraig and Lochore, there were two short branches in Dunfermline, one to the (perhaps appropriately named) Rumblingwell and the other to Townhill. The latter line involved a steep climb from Towngreen Toll, up Witch Loan (now better known as Townhill Road) to the small mining village which subsequently became a suburb of the town. Here tramcar 24 is standing at the Townhill terminus. Only the tramway line is paved, it being a condition of construction of any line that this was done.

A tramway was built to link Dunfermline and Rosyth, but opened too late (in May 1918) to be of much benefit to the war effort. Similarly, it was closed in July 1937, just too early to be of any use during the Second World War. This scene at the Rosyth terminus shows how much of the line was built on its own private right of way, creating no obstacle to road traffic and allowing the trams to reach (for that time) relatively high speeds.

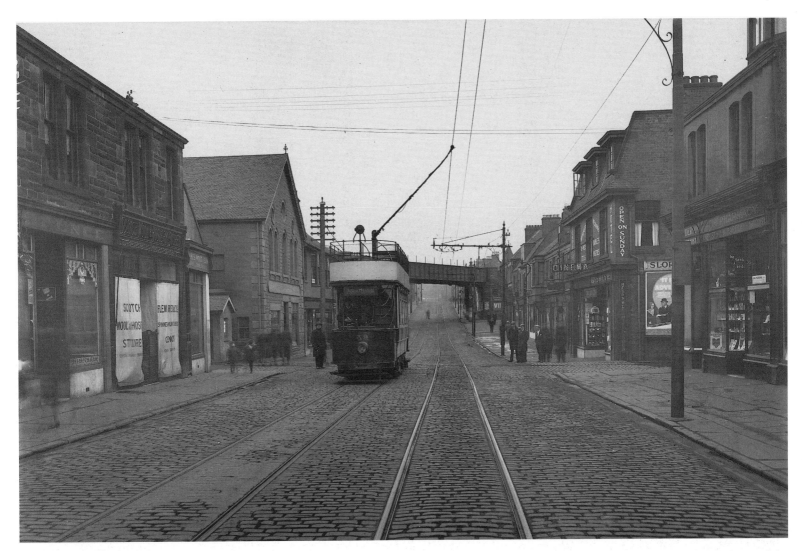

Cobblestones and tram rails in Cowdenbeath High Street. The tram en route for Lochore has stopped at the level crossing of the private railway of the Fife Coal Company. This was a source of much disruption to road traffic, and many attempts were made by Cowdenbeath Town Council to have it removed. However, the coal company pointed out that it was vital to their operations as it linked the pits to the west with the washery and main railway line to the east, and were the council to persist in its complaints numerous jobs would be lost. The line remained in place!

Construction of a new naval dockyard at Rosyth commenced before the outbreak of the First World War, but the complex took a number of years to complete. In common with most large construction projects at that time, the use of railways for the transport of materials was essential, and the site was covered with a labyrinth of tracks which had to be moved frequently as work proceeded. The main contractors, Messrs Easton Gibb & Son Ltd., employed at least 40 locomotives on the works, with hundreds of waggons. This loco has two numbers, Easton Gibb plate 80, and '15' stencilled on the cab side. It was built by Manning Wardle & Co. of Leeds, had been owned previously by Nuttall & Co., and was later sold to Cubitts. The train is the 'Pay Day Express', the weird shed on wheels in fact being the pay office!

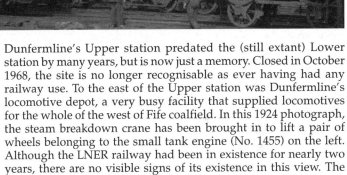

Dunfermline's Upper station predated the (still extant) Lower station by many years, but is now just a memory. Closed in October 1968, the site is no longer recognisable as ever having had any railway use. To the east of the Upper station was Dunfermline's locomotive depot, a very busy facility that supplied locomotives for the whole of the west of Fife coalfield. In this 1924 photograph, the steam breakdown crane has been brought in to lift a pair of wheels belonging to the small tank engine (No. 1455) on the left. Although the LNER railway had been in existence for nearly two years, there are no visible signs of its existence in this view. The locomotive depot was closed in 1967.

An engineer's inspection special train, photographed on 21 March 1914 near Aberdour. The line is on the large embankment built near the resort's White Sands (which with the passage of time have become the Silver Sands!). A stop has been made to permit somebody to descend from the single coach. The locomotive is one of the well-proportioned 4-4-2 tanks known as 'Yorkies', not from the now well-known chocolate bar but after their builders, the Yorkshire Engine Company of Meadowhall Works, Sheffield, which built numerous steam locomotives between 1866 and 1956. This one was less than three years old when photographed, later becoming LNER class C15.

The scattered nature of west Fife's villages resulted in the fairly early introduction of motor bus services. Prior to this a limited number of horse buses had been run from Dunfermline to places such as Culross, Lassodie and Lochgelly, but by contrast there was little available passenger railway service. The railways which criss-crossed this part of Fife were generally built for coal traffic only. The earliest motor bus service appears to have been a short-lived operation between Dunfermline and Cowdenbeath which did not survive the introduction of the trams. William Philp ran from the Abbey Gates to Saline and this picture shows his first bus, a 28-seat Straker–Squire (SP 891) in Saline Main Street, probably photographed in 1911 when it was new.

In the early 1920s the Dunfermline & District Tramways Company began to experience severe competition from 'pirate' buses which often ran just ahead of the trams to cream off their passengers. Eventually a degree of control was introduced by the local authorities, the outcome of which benefited the trams. Nevertheless the tramway company decided to introduce its own buses on other profitable routes. A large garage was built beside the St Leonard's tram depot and is seen here, probably in 1926. These Tilling Stevens buses had a petrol-electric drive (the petrol-fuelled engine drove an electric motor transmission). The bus side of the undertaking was run in close collaboration with the Scottish General Omnibus Co. of Larbert, as both were subsidiaries of the Fife Tramway Light & Power Company.

Several coachbuilders had premises in Dunfermline, and coachbuilding was one of many activities undertaken by Dunfermline Co-operative Society. This trailer, made to be pulled by its coal department's Fordson tractor, was a product of the local co-op body shop in 1928. Dunfermline's co-op was one of the earliest, founded in 1861, and was highly successful. It eventually had over 90 'outlet' departments distributed throughout the town and in outlying villages. 'Unitas House', the headquarters in Randolph Street, included several meeting rooms, a restaurant and a ballroom holding up to 600 people which played an important role in the lives of many burghers. It was a popular and well-remembered venue for wedding receptions.

Express delivery of boot and shoe repairs was accomplished by this motorcycle combination, of which the sidecar was built by the co-op's coachwork department. The bike itself is also a 'store' model, a 'Federation'. These were built by the Co-operative Wholesale Society in Tyseley, Birmingham, between 1919 and 1937, mostly from parts supplied by external suppliers. A bicycle, the 'Federal', was also made by the society in large numbers (the author's first bike was a Federal!). The store formed an amazingly large and complex organisation, and 'divvy' day would see treats purchased with the unaccustomed wealth of this early loyalty card scheme. The co-op's creamery in Pilmuir Street is in the background of this view.

BUY AT THE "STORE" IT PAYS.

COWDENBEATH

CO-OPERATIVE SOCIETY Lᵀᴰ.

'BAKERY

Dunfermline Co-op's coachbuilders also supplied goods to other societies, and this horse-drawn van was built in 1934 for the Cowdenbeath Co-op's bakery department. It was photographed in Burns Street, then not long built, and probably offering many inhabitants facilities such as inside toilets for the first time in their lives. The smaller neighbouring Kingseat and Townhill Co-ops were absorbed by the Dunfermline society in 1950 and 1957 respectively. Dunfermline Co-op's vehicles were always well turned out in Mid Brunswick Green with red wheels. Other co-ops used other colours, Townhill's vans being maroon and Cowdenbeath's dark red. Even small communities like Kingseat rose to operate their own individual societies.

Manclark Brothers, contractors of Forth Street, Dunfermline, bought this smart 3½ ton flatbed lorry from Albion Motors in October 1934. It is seen with a load of bricks from the local Lochside brickworks being used for new housing near Halbeath. The older single-storey housing on the right is typical of the miners' rows which once peppered this area, most of which were obliterated when opencast mining altered the surface features completely. Also worthy of note is the barrow on the left, specially designed for carrying bricks. Lochside brickworks at Townhill closed in 1974, having made many millions of bricks during its 70 year existence, in the process disposing of much waste from local pits.

Housing constructed in the 1920s and 30s tended to be fairly basic by modern standards, but was generally well-built and much has survived successive upgradings to form a large part of Fife's housing stock to this day. For most families it was the first move away from the miners' row and marked a vast improvement in living conditions. At one time the Fife Coal Company owned 3,500 houses but had a reputation for providing rather mediocre accommodation. After the Second World War, however, Mr R. W. Taylor was put in charge of an extensive improvement programme. This picture, showing Stenhouse Street in Cowdenbeath from the post office (now the Beath Stores), gives a good idea of how well-kept and quiet the streets were at a time when few working men could aspire to ownership of a motor car. Worthy of note is the unusual concrete (K1-236 type) telephone box, of a style produced between 1927 and 1930. These were superseded by the iconic and award-winning 1924 design of Sir Giles Gilbert Scott, the K2, the brief for which demanded that each box be produced for less than £40. The K2 was made of cast iron, with small, easily replaceable windows, and with the 'Jubilee' K6 variation of 1936 probably became as well-known a symbol of Britain as the red double deck bus was of London.

George Street in Cowdenbeath, situated off Stenhouse Street, photographed in the pre-war years when the only motor vehicles around were delivery lorries. Travelling shop vans became an important means of shopping as new housing was built further and further away from the traditional shopping centres, an example being this sole truck advertising 'Ripe Bananas' (without the now common 'greengrocers apostrophe'!). Note the lad at the left on the railings, observing the photographer from his vantage point. All these railings, and most from other areas, were soon to be uprooted for the scrap drive at the start of the Second World War. How much benefit this actually generated is very much open to debate, with most of the scrap gathered from these sources being unsuitable for reuse and left to rust in enormous stockpiles.

Dating from 1895, Bowhill Colliery was typical of the many pits in this part of west Fife. It was acquired by the Fife Coal Company in 1909 and was one of the deepest and most productive of its pits. Wheels in view range from those above the pithead to those on the many waggons; a necessary adjunct to any colliery for transporting the product to the customers. Despite a large investment in the mid-1950s to modernise Bowhill and increase output dramatically, the outlay was never recouped and it closed in 1965. On the left are the 'Hoffmann' style brick kilns which turned much of the colliery waste into a saleable product. One of the female brick workers can be seen at the right-hand end of the bank of kilns.

The pithead wheels are prominent in this view of Valleyfield Colliery, situated beside the Forth at Newmills between Culross and Torryburn. Established in 1906 by the Fife Coal Company, much of Valleyfield's output was initially sent to the coal-fired ships of the Royal Navy at Rosyth. A major modernisation scheme took place in 1954, and although the pit survived for more than two decades after this it closed in 1978. This part of Fife was the location of an interesting tale in the history of coal mining: when King James VI was taken down a pit at the water's edge, but was brought to the surface at the Moat Pit, on an island some distance from the shore, he thought he was being abducted!

John Jackson, another local coachbuilder, started his business in workshops in Mill Street, Dunfermline, in 1908 but moved to new premises in Pittencrieff Street in 1932. Specialising in bespoke bodywork and buses, that side of the business lost ground to Alexander of Falkirk after most bus companies came under their wing in the 1930s. This neat little twelve-seat bus, a Morris Commercial, was given its Jackson body and then photographed outside the Baldridgeburn Institute.

Jackson built other types of vehicles including this pneumatic-tyred flat, for horse haulage, for John Knox of Wester Gellet Farm. Wester Gellet is said to be the former name of what is now the Broomhall Estate. The Gellet Rock on the estate represents the height of the former limestone cliff prior to its excavation and burning in the Earl of Elgin's lime kilns. It is estimated that over ten million tons of stone have been quarried from this seam. East and West Gellet Farms lie to the west of the road from Dunfermline to Limekilns village, and the Gellet name is perpetuated in the name of the local historical society.

This Bentley 'S' series had a bespoke shooting brake body built by Jackson in the early 1950s for Alan Stewart of Wellfield.

Trams from Dunfermline to Lochore ceased operating on Sunday 4 July 1937. On the Monday morning, all the redundant vehicles were taken to the private track at the White Elephant pub at Hill of Beath in the hope that they could be sold on to another operator. In the event only one (No. 34) saw further use, in the unlikely setting of the tramway from Portrush to the Giant's Causeway in Northern Ireland. A great amount of work had to be done to make it suitable, and it was ultimately little used there. After sitting (unvandalised!) for some weeks, all the other cars were sold and taken to Kinghorn to form holiday chalets on the site of the former shipyard there. They did not last long in this guise, but two were then taken to Pettycur Bay where they remained until the 1960s. The two long single-deck cars in this view had started life with the Wemyss & District Tramways Company, but were not much used in Dunfermline.

St David's harbour was a transport time warp with conditions little changed in 150 years. This photograph of a horse-drawn waggon taking coal to the small privately owned harbour was taken in July 1946. The last export was shipped just a month later, on 10 August. The harbour was built by the Hendersons, owners of the Fordel Estate, for their exclusive use in the 1750s and remained in their hands until the end of coal export. It then became a shipbreaking and scrap yard, and has seen a remarkable regeneration in recent years as part of the extending new township of Dalgety Bay. The harbour is now surrounded by modern flats, the like of which could never have been imagined 50 years ago. Unfortunately it is not used as a haven or yacht marina, a feature which would now add greatly to its charm. Around the new footpath by the harbour can be found old stone sleepers, a relic of the former waggonway.

4143 | Limekilns, West.

An Alexander single-deck Leyland photographed in the 1930s on the then newly reconstructed road along the waterfront at Halkett's Hall, Limekilns. The name recalls the Halkett family, early landowners in the area. This photograph was taken from near the landward end of Limekilns pier, which served as the point of export for a considerable tonnage of coal, brought to the pier by waggonway from 1773 until 1809. In the left distance are the cranes of the ship-breaking yard of Messrs Shipbreaking Industries Ltd., active at Charlestown harbour from 1923 until 1963. The last vessels to be reduced to their component parts at the harbour were submarines, with the dismantling of the very last, HMS *Searcher*, commencing in October 1962. **39**

Following the withdrawal of the trams, most of the tracks were quickly lifted as this view of Cowdenbeath High Street shows, although the overhead support poles, typified by that on the right, remained in place for a number of years. This photograph was taken from almost the same spot as the one on page 23, and the amount of road traffic is on the increase, although still light compared with today's volumes. Cowdenbeath High Street formed part of the A9, the main road north from Queensferry to Perth and Inverness, a route now dramatically improved by virtue of the motorway network through Fife and upgraded roads beyond allowing journeys to be completed in a fraction of the time required by intrepid motorists of the 1930s.

Main Street, Glencraig, in the late 1930s, with the village's 'Gothenburg' Tavern on the right. The Swedish city gave its name to a licensing system, adopted in parts of Britain, whereby 'Goths' (as the pubs were known) were licensed by the local authority with profits ploughed back into the community. This was the last mining village on the line before the tram reached its terminus in Lochore. Here also the tram rails have been speedily removed, but the poles which formerly carried the overhead power supply wires remain, now only carrying small electric street lamps. One of the new double deck buses is heading for Dunfermline. The view is totally unrecognisable today as none of these buildings – which formed the heart of this mining village – have survived the 'beautification' of the former industrial landscape.

St David's found a role in the post-war economy when the National Coal Board located a yard for the construction of an offshore drilling platform there in 1956–7. This platform was used to verify the coal reserves in the Forth off Kirkcaldy and Culross and the NCB's contractors established a base at Torryburn, with caravans used as temporary accommodation for the itinerant workers. The strange vehicle in the centre is a DUKW, an amphibious craft used to gain access to the platform in the middle of the river. It was designed for a military role and could carry up to 25 soldiers and their equipment in war conditions.

The DUKW takes to the water. DUKWs were designed for the US army by Col. Frank Speir and were first used on Operation Husky, the invasion of Sicily in 1943. The 2½ ton 6-wheeled vehicle featured a hollow airtight body, plus a propeller for propulsion in water, and could achieve 50 mph on land or 5 knots afloat. Some 20,000 were constructed by General Motors Corporation, the strange name (which by good fortune sounded similar to 'duck'), being derived from its GM code: D = the first year of production (1942); U = body style (Utility / Amphibious); K = all-wheel drive; W = dual rear axle. Today waterborne tours on DUKWs can be experienced in Boston and Sydney harbours.

This photograph is captioned 'Demonstration at Blairhall Colliery' and probably relates to the delivery of wooden pit props in a manner that allowed them to be offloaded by forklift, rather than manhandled. Note yet more wheels at the side, in this case an upside-down mine tub of the type then in use at Blairhall, a fairly advanced design for the time. Much surface-level coal handling was done by conveyor, as illustrated by the modern structures behind the Leyland lorry.

As described earlier, Dunfermline Co-operative Society built the bodywork for most of its large fleet of specialist vehicles. This co-op baker's van – a big improvement on Allan's horse-van seen on page 19 – had stopped in Whinney Knowe, North Queensferry, within sight of the rail bridge, when this snap of Mrs Jack (left) and Mrs Anderson was taken as they put the world to rights.

Dunfermline had two bus stations, with the lower one located in St Margaret's Street. The town's other, or top, bus station was in Carnegie Street, an inconvenient walk away, particularly on a wet day. Unattractive serried rows of shelters with corrugated asbestos roofs did nothing to lift the spirits when one arrived, although Jack Drummond's snack bar provided a welcome cup of something hot on a cold winter's day. The unusual building on the corner of Chapel Street opposite was built as a model lodging house in the nineteenth century, and had separate entrances for male and female occupants. After it ceased to be used for this purpose the upper storey eventually became a makeshift recording studio, with a boxing club below. A recent fire in a furniture store, occupying another part of the building, has put its future in jeopardy. Both bus stations were closed following construction of a brand new purpose-built terminal for all services, opened as an integral part of the Kingdom Shopping Centre in 1984.

Buses for Blairhall and Solsgirth Mine wait for passengers at the top bus stance *c*.1974. The vehicles are, on the left, Leyland PSU3 single deck WXA 942M of 1973, and on the right Daimler CRG6 double deck SXA 64K which dated from two years earlier. The XA registration (originally used by London) was issued by Kirkcaldy for ten years after 1963. Flares were the height of fashion then . . . undoubtedly some of today's extreme fashions will seem just as outmoded in a short time.

Occasionally tall vehicles have come to grief at the area's low bridges. This Alexander vehicle (RO 598) gave itself a headache at Burntisland docks, and the driver would no doubt have received more than that when he was reprimanded for the damage caused. Signs on this bridge indicate that the clearance is just 13 feet, although the structure just to the east, leading to the shipyard, is 2' 9" higher and would probably have been adequate for the bus to pass safely under.